How India's atheist movement shaped my life

Dr Keerthi

Copyright © 2024 by Dr Keerthi

All rights reserved.

This book or any portion thereof may not be reproduced or used in any manner whatsoever without the express written permission of the respective writer of the respective content except for the use of brief quotations in a book review.

The writer of the respective work holds sole responsibility for the originality of the content and IndiePress is not responsible in any way whatsoever.

Printed in India

IndiePress

ISBN: 978-93-6045-006-9

First Printing, 2024

IndiePress

A division of Nasadiya Technologies Private Ltd.

Koramangala, Bangalore

Karnataka-560029

http://indiepress.in/

Typeset by Zoheb Ahmed

Book Cover designed by Keerthipriya PH

Publishing Consultant – Zoheb Ahmed

Contents

Introduction 1

Chapter 1 9

Chapter 2 23

Chapter 3 33

Chapter 4 43

Chapter 5 63

The author Keerthi with her grandfather Gora

Introduction

Someone asked me why I decided to share my life story. I replied: because nowadays religion has infiltrated every aspect of our lives to our disadvantage.

In present day India, I could be trolled or worse, for saying that religion is holding down our country. And that brings me to my second reason.

Our democracy is in danger.

Don't get me wrong. I'm not suggesting that India will no longer be a democracy if the country continues down the path it is presently treading but we will have lost the spirit that symbolises a true democracy. Democracy doesn't just bequeath the right to elect your government. Democracy means to vote freely. Democracy means to live freely. To accept people with differing views.

Today, more than ever, I see people shackled by concepts that discourage free and rational thinking. These concepts are packaged in religion. But this book isn't about bashing religion. It's about exhorting individuals to think for themselves.

My motive isn't to broadcast my life's highs and lows but to share the ideology that shaped my life, and show it is conducive to preserving the spirit of democracy as well as to living life fully.

That ideology is atheism. Also referred to as humanism or rationalism, especially in the West.

Atheism is commonly understood to be the absence of a belief in God. While that is true, what's more important is the foundation for that belief—the atheist outlook that every living being is equal.

Essentially, there is no supernatural power beyond life on this earth.

Equality entitles everyone to his or her say, his or her life, as long as it does not impinge on my own right to live.

Articles 14 to 18 of the Indian Constitution lay down the right to equality. Article 14 grants every individual equality before law. Article 15 prohibits discrimination on the basis of religion, race, caste, gender or place of birth. Article 16 confers equal opportunities in public employment. Article 17 abolishes untouchability while Article 18 abolishes titles.

Most people will not need to look far to realise that those Articles aren't being implemented in real life.

How many girls and women have never been discriminated against at home, or in an educational institution, or at the workplace?

So many girls are compelled to drop out of school on hitting puberty because their faith limits their existence to bearing children and household chores. Keeping girls and women away from education and the workforce is as much a loss to themselves as it is to the nation. So many women aren't allowed to express themselves at home let alone participate in crucial family decisions or access family finance. So many widows suffer at the hands of society and have to follow ridiculous rules such as not being allowed to wear a *bindi (sindhu/kumkum)*, not being seen in the morning and not being allowed to attend ceremonies.

How many people from minority religions haven't been discriminated against in educational institutions or at workplaces?

And how many people of tribal origin or from lower castes haven't been discriminated against likewise?

I remember visiting a few government schools in the early days of my social service career. I was stunned to see how the class attendance had been marked on the blackboard. If the class had 100 students, the attendance was marked somewhat like this:

| General: 37 |
| SC: 14 |
| ST: 9 |
| OBC: 21 |
| Absent: |
| Total: 100 |

I failed to understand why the attendance was marked by caste. It was as though the caste concept was being drilled into the minds of children. For sure those children would grow up to be caste-conscious adults.

I know of colleges where students group together by caste. Serious differences of opinions between such groups sometimes cause clashes, which political leaders milk for whatever gains (read 'votes') they can garner.

The preamble of our Constitution endorses secularism. I studied in a secular institution run by a group of atheists. It was a beautiful experience. I'm convinced it's the best way to learn that we are one.

Our towns and cities have *harijan wadas*—places inhabited by people called *harijans*, literally meaning 'people of God' but used to refer to the lowest social caste among Hindus. In modern parlance these places are called colonies of people belonging to scheduled castes or scheduled tribes. In Andhra Pradesh, the state I'm from, we have corporations established by the government for people belonging to different castes, so you have Kapu corporation, Gowda corporation and so on. These groups then become vote banks. Their leaders clamour for benefits for their members, not for everyone.

My life has shown me that those believing in equality don't treat the female gender as subservient to the male gender. Those believing in equality don't treat people born in a certain caste as untouchable. Nor do they believe that those people must remain untouchable.

Caste and religion have so far been passed on from one generation to the next. Remarkably, nowadays, people from 'so-called' castes are happy to register their children as members of the same caste for the sake of availing reservations. I don't find this self-serving but selfish because it precludes children from figuring out the world for themselves. In my view, children are born without a stamp of caste and religion. They should make their own decisions as they navigate this world.

My maternal grandfather Goparaju Ramachandra Rao (he went by the name Gora, an acronym composed of the first two letters in his family name and the first two letters in his given name), the founder of the atheist movement in India, spent time with learned people from every religion (including Mahatma Gandhi) and read every scripture he could lay his hands on.

"Capture the goodness in each," he would exhort us children. "Question every social practice that goes against equality."

A popular saying among those practicing Islam is "inshallah." If Allah wills it. But what if you take God out the equation?

Who wills anything then?

When you take God out the equation, you need to question to get answers. So, as children, when we fell, we were advised to figure out what we had done wrong and how we could right that wrong. We had to take responsibility for ourselves.

Atheists don't pass the buck for their troubles to God.

As children, we were taught to question and to think rationally. Questioning brings clarity. Questioning allows you to explore radical solutions to the problems ailing society. Questioning is at the heart of a democracy. But today, any sort of questioning is being discouraged. People who dare to question are being put away. Not just ordinary citizens but also parliamentarians and legislators face punitive action for airing their opinion and wanting debates on matters concerning the public.

Today, we're seeing political parties with different manifestos entering into a coalition to form a government. They want to save our democracy.

My grandfather Gora favoured a partyless democracy. Does India have individuals who are principled and value-driven, who offer to represent a potential electorate? Equally important, are Indians sufficiently committed to values to want such righteous leaders?

Today, decisions taken both by families and communities are driven by religion and caste not by merit and facts. On social media, caste and religion have become attributes to flaunt as well as criticise. We see people practicing a certain faith or belonging to a certain caste being given derogatory labels.

Why? When our Constitution tells us to respect every individual for who he or she is?

Good people come from all religions. Likewise, people performing criminal acts come from every religion. You cannot generalise. Differences can be discussed, dialogues are healthy.

Sadly, religion has also become a pivot for politics. We routinely see seats being allocated on the basis of religion and caste instead of capability and efficiency.

Some religious leaders, in turn, support political parties that espouse their expansion. This reduces the whole idea of democracy to zero.

How can that be good for the country? Such practices influence our youth, and make them more conscious of religion and caste.

A few broad-minded younger members of society are entering into inter-faith or inter-caste marriages even against the wishes of their parents. That's a positive sign. But after the marriage, sometimes, one partner tries to force the other into converting. Why? What happened to their 'love'?

Religious conversion is not new to India. It's been happening since decades. People offer social support to those facing social or economic challenges to encourage them to convert. Why should you want to convert another person's religion? Someone facing a challenge may need material help or counselling. Such moments shouldn't be used as instances to convert a person.

Religion is a private matter. It should remain so.

As time goes by, religion and caste are becoming a stronger influence on society and weakening our democracy.

If religion is truly about peace, why does it frequently become a bone of contention between communities?

If religion is about peace, no criminal should be a believer. But they claim to belong to one faith or the other. How is that so?

Couples marry on auspicious days at auspicious times. Despite that, relationships fall apart. Why? Why don't the stars protect them?

Couples take solemn marital vows prescribed by their religion. Still they hurt one another. Why? If they could "follow" their religion for the sake of taking their marriage vows, why can't they "follow" their religion for the sake of fulfilling those vows?

My second husband regularly visited temples and went through months of special worship. He was very religious. But he cheated me as well as abused me. Of what use is religion if it doesn't serve as a moral compass for your life?

I'm the last person to want to convert anyone. But it's worth asking: has my religion been reduced to symbolism? To lighting *diyas* and bursting fireworks on Diwali? To exchanging presents and cutting a cake at Christmas? To fasting and feasting through Ramadaan?

What values am I practicing in life?

Am I emphasising humanity over a dogmatic practice of religion?

If my words can encourage even one person to widen his or her horizon this effort will be worth it. *Jai Insaan!* Hail humanity!

Chapter 1

They say behind every successful man is a woman. What about every successful woman? Who stands behind her?

I'd say: her family.

I can pinpoint my family as the singular reason for my success. Don't get me wrong. I'm not a celebrity by any means but I say with confidence that I took every adversity life threw at me in my stride. I found the strength to deal with life's curveballs. I trace this ability to the beliefs my family ingrained in me.

Your beliefs shape your world view. Your world view, in turn, becomes a foundation for the decisions you take in life.

I was taught early on that I am responsible for my life.

I was 13 when my grandfather Gora released a book called *Positive Atheism*.

Until then, all I knew about atheism was that we (aka my family) didn't perform *"puja"* like my friends and their families. Nor did we celebrate Hindu festivals like Holi, Diwali and so on. Having said that, it wasn't as if we lived in isolation. I used to visit my friends on festive days and for events like marriages. I simply considered such gatherings to be social dos.

I never felt the urge to ask my friends about their religious beliefs. Life was good, and so, everything that my family elders had taught me made sense!

In fact, by the time I faced hardship later in life, atheism had become a part of me. Thinking for myself had become my way of life. Blaming a supernatural power for my hardship or asking that supernatural power for help didn't make sense.

Also, as I grew, I became aware that some so-called believers got involved with anti-social activities, some petty, some downright criminal. I used to wonder if religion meant merely reading a scripture or saying a prayer? Else, how did the so-called believers justify their actions?

As a child, I had never been introduced to God nor had God ever come up in conversations with my family. But, when my grandfather released *Positive Atheism* in 1972, he made it a point to read it out, chapter by chapter, to all his grandchildren—my three siblings (I have two sisters and a brother), my nine cousins and myself.

Grandfather would repeatedly say: Take responsibility for your actions. Don't try to pass the buck to God. Or anyone else. And if something untoward happens as a result of something you have done, then too, take responsibility for the adverse outcome.

Grandfather had turned to atheism after being unable to find a rational reason for the propagation of social inequities in Hinduism, his religion by birth. He had lived by atheist principles, principles he believed in so strongly that he went on to found the world's first Atheist Centre in Vijayawada, in Andhra Pradesh, India. When we were young, he saw it fit to inculcate those ideals in his grandchildren.

This paragraph from *An Atheist with Gandhi*, a book based on grandfather's conversations with the Mahatma (released in 1951), briefly summarises what drew grandfather to atheism:

I want atheism, so that man shall cease to depend on god and stand firmly on his own legs. In such a man a healthy social outlook will grow, because atheism finds no justification for the economic and social inequalities between man and man.

That same year, on the Silver Jubilee of India's Independence Day, grandfather arranged a "beef and pork meet" to further acceptance for different dietary preferences. He shunned religious diktats on diet. I vividly recall participating in that event and eating tiny portions of the different meats served to express solidarity with the cause.

At home, we were served both vegetarian as well as non-vegetarian food. A typical meal would include legumes, a green leafy vegetable, rice, fruit, a dairy product and groundnuts. Occasionally, we were served sorghum rice. Non-vegetarian food was served on Sunday or on festive days.

Father would encourage us to eat seasonal vegetables and fruit. "It's nature's bounty for the present moment," he would say. "Eat it and stay healthy."

However, we weren't forced to eat anything. We chose what to eat based on our individual preferences.

Grandfather was a great one for growing more edible produce instead of flowers.

"India needs to grow more fruit and vegetables than flowers," he'd say. "Of what use are flowers in comparison to fruit and vegetables?"

Grandfather actually inspired the celebration of "a day of fruit and vegetables" across the state, an event that drew the (then) deputy chief minister of Andhra Pradesh BV Subba Reddy.

People were encouraged to exchange fruit bouquets instead of regular ones and garlands made of fruit and vegetables instead of flowers.

Gora was a doer, not a preacher. He led by example.

We were taught that all life, all living beings are equal, plants, animals and humans. We were told that death is final, that no spirit outlives the body. We practiced no rituals after the death of a family member. We usually donated the bodily parts of family members who died to medical colleges, although a few family members were cremated in an electric crematorium after they passed.

Consequently, I neither believe in rebirth nor in reincarnation.

In essence, atheism was introduced to me in a very positive way. It honed a positive outlook on life in me.

What helped deepen my belief in atheism was the fact that my friends accepted my family's way of thinking. Their acceptance partly stemmed from the fact that my family was deeply engaged with social work. We were seen as good people, as people to support and appreciate. It sounds simple but it's actually a deep statement.

If you define people as "good" or "bad," simply on the basis of what they do, their beliefs or the family they were born to ceases to become a reason for social divisions.

Atheism taught me that humanity is one. That's a powerful lesson to carry you through life.

*

Being atheist and thinking rationally go hand in hand. As much as Gora led his family (and countless others) to embrace atheism to overrule societal divisions, he also pushed us to think about what we thought, what we believed in, what we said and what we did.

In the early 1970s when Andhra Pradesh was seeing a lot of political unrest which caused the protracted closure of educational institutions, Gora had taken it upon himself to teach his grandchildren.

One time he assigned me an essay about a love story he had read out from our English text. It was your typical love story with a happy ending.

I thought I would make a good impression on grandfather by starting the essay with a quotation, a practice my teacher had told me would fetch a higher score.

Now the only quote I knew on love was 'love is blind.' "It doesn't matter," I thought. "It'll work ... "

Of course it didn't. Grandfather pulled me up for using a phrase out of turn.

"Why did you write that love is blind? What was blind about their love? Think about what you say."

Grandfather literally squeezed out any iota of blind faith we harboured within. I loved the way he pushed us to think. He wanted us to be aware, not blind! All the while, he remained open to learning from us if we had something meaningful to add to any discussion.

Rationalism meant that reason—sound logic—dictated every family decision. For instance, none of the children in the family were given names that their parents fancied. We were all named after a real situation that had transpired around the time of our birth.

My maternal uncle Lavanam (meaning 'salt' in Telugu) got his name from Mahatma Gandhi's salt satyagrah that was underway when he was born in 1930. My mother Vidya (meaning 'knowledge') was born in 1934 when Gandhi introduced basic education. Niyanta (meaning 'dictator') was born in 1943 during the second world war propagated by dictators like Hitler and Mussolini. Nau (meaning 'nine') was grandfather's ninth child.

Grandfather was once asked what he might have named his tenth and eleventh born children, had he had two more. He quipped: "Das (meaning 'ten') and Bas (meaning 'stop')."

I was named Keerthi (meaning 'famous') because around October 1955, when I was born, my maternal uncle Lavanam, who was touring India with Vinoba Bhave (the leader of the Bhoodan Movement) as his personal (volunteer) translator, gained public recognition for his work.

Grandfather himself dropped his family name Goparaju and his given name Ramachandra Rao in lieu of Gora.

*

Growing up in Patamata Lanka, a village near Vijayawada, I was quite young when I became aware that women were rarely seen on the streets. Whereas men worked and sat around chatting in the evenings, women stayed indoors and occupied themselves with household chores.

Women would never show their face to a man who wasn't a family member. If we visited so-and-so auntie's place, aunty wouldn't step into the room my father sat in. She would stand outside the door with a serving tray, and let any of the men in her family or a servant take the tray from her hands and serve the guests.

One time when a road was being laid to connect our village with a main road, the local authority called upon the community to assist. My parents, my grandparents, my brothers and sisters, we all did our bit. But our family stood out like a sore thumb in the sea of men who had turned up to assist. No other women or girls had showed up. When we got back home, I recall my parents talking about the situation.

At home, it was normal for father and other men in the family to pitch in with house-work, be it sweeping the floor or washing kitchen utensils. Father in particular would chop veggies every morning.

My sisters and brother and I were treated the same. None of the elders in our family designated certain tasks as girl's work and certain tasks as boy's work. All of us would be assigned work in the garden, cooking, cleaning and so on.

At the special school we attended, special because grandfather had established Vasavya Vidyalayam to propagate his belief system, and my aunts and uncle managed it, our teachers never differentiated between boys and girls. Boys as well as girls were assigned chores such as cleaning the campus, refilling drinking water sources and so on.

Father certainly didn't believe that women were to be confined indoors. Mother was only 15 when she got married. Father encouraged her to sit for the matriculation exam, and thereafter get a pre-university certificate and a degree in sociology. "As you grow, society will grow," he used to say.

Father also encouraged mother to accept a nomination to the position of ex officio member of the Gollapudi panchayat at the age of 21, and he stood by her when she was selected by the Congress political party to contest the Vijayawada parliamentary seat at the age of 42.

Father was behind mother when she launched Vasavya Mahila Mandali, the social organisation I now head. Essentially, father stood by her every step of the way. I didn't realise it then, but the way father treated mother became the bar by which I would judge men in future.

Not only father but my paternal grandmother also encouraged mother to grow. Grandmother would engage my siblings and me to give mother time to study. She would help mother by making her endless cups of coffee and readying her bath water. On an examination day she would see off mother with a hug and a kiss, and bless her. She would anxiously wait for mother to return. If mother came home lamenting that the exam had been tough, grandmother would motivate her, saying: "I'm sure you will pass," and then encourage mother to study for the next exam.

Grandmother would welcome mother as lovingly when she returned late at night from her work in the district. When mother was elected as a member of parliament from Vijayawada in 1980, grandmother sobbed. They were tears of pride. I don't recollect ever hearing mother and grandmother argue or criticise each other.

As much as my parents' relationship echoed gender equality, my paternal grandmother's plight echoed gender inequality. She had been widowed when father was 13 years old.

Grandfather had been broken by the loss of an orange crop to pests. The thought that he wouldn't be able to repay the debt agonised him. He had crumbled both physically and psychologically, and succumbed soon after.

After losing her husband, grandmother took to dairy farming to earn a livelihood. My aunts, father's two elder sisters supported their mother by weaving cotton and managing a kitchen garden. My father and his older brother dropped out of school and joined an automobile mechanic unit in Vijayawada. They walked 10 kilometres to work and back. Money was tight but the family managed.

My perspective was simple: "The family suffered the loss, not just grandfather. But he went to pieces, not grandmother. So surely, she was tough, perhaps of stronger mettle than he?"

Still, as far back as I can remember, I had always seen grandmother dressed in a coarse white sari with no blouse, no ornaments, no *bindi*, her hair tied in a simple knot without any flowers... she was the epitome of renunciation. It bothered me that widows were compelled to "show" their widowhood but men who lost their wife were free to do as they pleased. It bothered me that a woman who had worked hard to make ends meet after being widowed at an early age wasn't respected for her skills. It also bothered me that men in general, didn't allow their wives to progress. My mother and aunts used to hold adult education classes for tribal women, to help them become financially independent. One night, I remember a woman came in with a bleeding gash on her head. Her husband had hit her with an axe because she had read aloud a sign on a bus... he was illiterate and couldn't take his wife getting ahead of him. I was saddened to think of the sick mentality behind the gruesome act, and the extent to which a man could go to put down a woman.

The more gender inequality I saw in society, the more I got attracted to Gora's atheist teachings.

*

Growing up, I had never heard a family elder identify a person by his or her caste or religion. Consequently, caste and religion were beyond my social radar.

At home, father would ensure that our house help Gopayya sat with us every evening to study English and Telugu and maths. We were made to understand that Gopayya's life circumstances had made him a house help but in no way did that mean that he couldn't learn basic life skills sitting in our company.

Thanks to grandfather, we took part in *padyatras* (foot marches usually undertaken for a cause) as children. We would walk with our family members. These events introduced us to social disparities and the need to stand up to the political establishment to fight social injustice.

We were also exposed to meaningful cultural activities and encouraged to take part in those. I vividly recollect a dance ballet that showed brightness on the one side and darkness on the other. The bright represented the "haves" of society. The darkness represented the "have not's." I learned a lot from that dance and other events. It was unlike much of the entertainment one sees today.

At school, my siblings and I engaged with our classmates without caring about their caste and religion. My friends knew that we didn't care for caste or religious symbolism. So we never spoke about those matters let alone come into conflict about them.

In fact, our school organised special events to help us shed any discriminatory outlook we might have picked up from home or society. On a certain day, every child would bring his or her own tiffin plus extra food for one more child. Our teachers would pool this food. The idea was—students must consume food from each other's homes so that no child is discriminated against.

*

I was very young when I realised that a lot of people of all ages would walk into our home for various kinds of assistance. As many homes in our village didn't have electricity supply, many students would visit our home in the evening after sunset to study.

A group of teenage boys would drop in once weekly for a meal. Father and a few other villagers were jointly sponsoring their education and accommodation.

Father would go out of his way to find children desirous of studying further but without the means to do so. When I was seven, he was appointed a non-official member in a government-run Industrial Training Institute in Vijayawada. Father would ask for a list of students who had been selected but who couldn't afford the fee. He would write them postcards, asking them to meet him. Many would turn up at home in the days after. Father would counsel them, talk to their parents and instruct one of his workers to pay their fees. Being privy to these meetings and decisions impressed on me the value of sponsoring a person's education to help him (or her) lead a life of dignity.

Decades later when mother was a member of parliament, she once visited the head office of Engineers Institute Limited in New Delhi, as a member of a parliamentary committee. There she met an officer who asked her if she knew Chennupati Seshagiri Rao.

"I am his wife," said mother.

The officer told her that in 1962 he had studied at the Industrial Training Institute in Vijayawada thanks to father's support. The man had still kept the postcard that Chennupati Seshagiri Rao had written him. After a couple of months, he brought his family to visit father. It was humbling to see him touch father's feet and express his gratitude.

"Mr Rao," he said. "I would like to give you a contract in gratitude for your help twenty years ago."

"I would be happy if you would educate at least one person and help him find employment," replied father.

Mother's way of showing us what was important was to involve us in social initiatives. Our family would run two buses to ferry young women enrolled at the Maris Stella College in Vijayawada to college and back home. Many of those young women were allowed to attend college only because of the safe transportation my family provided. Mother would get my siblings and me to make out receipts for the nominal sums the young women paid for the service. We could see that the collection didn't cover the cost. It was another subtle demonstration of the need to give back to society.

My maternal grandmother was a champion of pregnant women from poor families. She would give them a glass of milk and curd. She enlisted our help to churn curd to make buttermilk.

We were one of the first families to have a telephone at home. That too, was treated like a community asset. We routinely received calls for so-and-so villager and we would be sent off to summon the villager to receive a second call, or to pass on a message.

Years later when mother was elected a member of parliament, the first thing she prioritised was a public phone in the post office. She got me to make a list of villages needing a public telephone and collect letters from each panchayat to kick-start the process.

*

When I was six, a male servant took me to the first floor of our home and asked me to remove my underwear. Then, he sexually abused me.

I have no idea why I didn't tell my mother and my grandmother about the incident. Perhaps because I didn't understand what had happened to me until I was a teen? And by then, I may have thought it was too late to bring up the matter so I kept quiet about that unfortunate episode.

So why am I now writing about being sexually abused as a child?

As a responsible citizen I think I should be open about incidents that could help a parent protect a child. Yes, I know it is commonly said that children should be made aware of "good touch" and "bad touch" to help protect them from abuse. I think those words are being used too loosely. I think we should be using animation and video content more than just telling children. It would be more effective.

I also feel that parents and guardians need to be taught how to recognise tell-tale signs of a child who might have been abused or who wants to express a painful thought. Children don't go around maligning a servant or an uncle. If they suggest some such thing, it is up to the guardian to probe the matter.

I've seen that children are often ignored or not encouraged when they want to say something. Sometimes, parents don't believe their children. Also, parents tend to trust those around implicitly. The servant who sexually abused me was almost a part of our family. Most child sexual abusers have special access to the child. They may have been entrusted with the care of the child. They abuse that trust.

*

I was in awe of father through my childhood. He was a disciplinarian in every sense of the word, setting a strong work conduct, punctuality code, dress code, you name it, he set it.

"You should manage time, not allow time to manage you," he'd say.

I deeply admired and respected father, he taught us so much just by being the man he was.

Mother was the epitome of patience. No matter what happened, she would never get rattled. Mother spent a lot of time outdoors because she was politically and socially active. Nevertheless, she more than made up for her absence by the depth of her engagement with us, her children. While my maternal grandmother would fill in for mother in many ways, mother made sure that she knew what was going on in our minds. We would freely share our aspirations with her and she would support us to fulfil our dreams.

When I was a child, I used to aspire to become "a doctor to serve the nation at the borders" or "a newsreader because I was impressed by the anchor's voice and pronunciation."

My parents used to encourage me to become whatever I wanted. But my poor score in mathematics in my matriculate exam—I got 39 per cent—thwarted my dream of studying medicine. So I resorted to Plan B. I studied English literature at the intermediate level, during which time I decided I would become a professional social worker. So I chose appropriate subjects at the graduate level and when father showed reluctance to send me to Vishakapatnam for a post graduate degree, mother stepped in to ease the way.

I owe my family for making me the person I am. They gave me everything I could possibly need to lead a good life, and I don't mean that in the materialistic sense.

Chapter 2

I don't equate education with the prefixes and suffixes bequeathed by the successful completion of a degree. For me, education has a broader meaning. I see education as the acquisition of life skills, as acquiring knowledge about one's surroundings and developing a positive attitude towards the world. Empathy for other people, sensitivity towards their plight, respect for every living creature, civic sense, these are essential outcomes of education. You can't live well without discipline, and that's something you develop through education.

I don't correlate education with educational institutions. My father had no degree but his time management skills were exemplary. He was a school dropout but he could plan and schedule and run a business employing many. People got attracted to him and looked to him to lead the way because of his behaviour. Where did father learn those life skills?

We learn a lot in school and college. Not just the subjects we study but also about right and wrong, and how to manage ourselves. But we can learn as much by being observant in the presence of those who know.

The fact that father was considered successful by worldly standards impressed on me the importance of being a sponge, of being able to glean from every opportunity to learn. In my time, we had no internet to browse the world wide web. We expanded our horizons by reading, listening to the radio and in my instance, by keenly listening to the foreigners who visited my grandfather. Until today I haven't seen a parallel to their strong civic sense and their passion to take their country forward.

I don't associate getting an education with any particular age. It's a lifelong process as long as you stay open to learning and to updating yourself. I studied in France when I was in my fifties. And, only yesterday I signed up for a course on counselling women facing menopause. Who says you can't learn even at 69?

I correlate education with growth. I credit that perspective to the special school my siblings and I attended. Special because grandfather had established Vasavya Vidyalayam to propagate the concepts he believed in. His children, my aunts and uncle managed the school.

At Vasavya Vidyalayam, teachers didn't differentiate between boys and girls. Boys as well as girls were assigned chores such as cleaning the campus, refilling drinking water sources and so on.

At Vasavya Vidyalayam, my siblings and I engaged with our classmates without caring about their caste and religion. We never spoke about those matters let alone come into conflict about them. We were encouraged to shed discriminatory outlooks we may have picked up at home.

I loved school because it gave me space to grow. We had ample opportunity to draw, design, experiment and ask. Our drawing classes were held outdoors and we were assigned real sceneries to draw. We were never bogged down with home-work.

Contrary to the widely prevailing custom of putting teachers on a pedestal, at Vasavya Vidyalaya, teachers and students alike sat on gunny bags on the floor. Both the teachers and the students wore a uniform made of *khadi* (homespun coarse cotton cloth). We were encouraged to share our ideas and lead the organisation of school events. One day a week was dedicated to creative classes. We were exposed to the thoughts of overseas visitors to grandfather's atheist centre. My aunt used to read to us about inspiring personalities. I was especially inspired by the life of Helen Keller.

Vasavya Vidyalaya was a school with a difference, imparting ideas that were hard to come about in those days.

When I was 14-years-old, I enrolled at the Maris Stella College in Vijayawada, a college for girls managed by Catholic Christian missionaries. My family had brought me up as an atheist but made it very clear that I lived in a multicultural, pluralistic society, and I had to respect as well as tolerate other people's faiths. Atheism had given me a solid grounding in that understanding, in accepting every living being as being equally entitled to the universe. So, not only did I fit into the college milieu very rapidly, I was also able to appreciate the value that the nuns brought to the institution.

Not once did I feel that the nuns heading the institution were out to impose their faith on us. For sure, their faith gave them a lot of discipline, and certainly, they wanted us to become more disciplined. My father had already tutored me in the basics of discipline. But the nuns polished our manners no end. For instance, I was taken aback when I was first told that when I stood in class to greet a lecturer, it wasn't acceptable to push back my chair noisily. I had to stand up without making any screeching sound.

Despite their staunch faith and their (might I say) "saintly"" lifestyle, our principal and vice principal were very understanding. We were free to choose the dances and songs we wanted to perform at college events. They accepted our cultural preferences without any fuss. In fact, our vice principal, despite being a nun, had an excellent dress sense and she would go out of her way to help us pick the right dresses for our performances.

Their openness helped me become more broad-minded. So when we had to recite a Catholic prayer during assembly, and end with the word "Amen," I was okay. I didn't get upset. And just before Christmas, when they asked us to contribute a few gifts to distribute to the poor,

I saw their actions from the charity point of view. I appreciated their missionary zeal to serve the destitute. I didn't see it as a religious thing.

Being a missionary run college, moral science was a compulsory subject. That was a new for me. Atheism had introduced me to morality as ethics. We had no concept of divine law or divine punishment. Our understanding of right and wrong was beyond religion.

The nun who took our moral science class would tell us stories to nudge us to understand morality, and to influence our behaviour at large.

I remember one such lesson:

An elderly woman is trying to cross a road. She's carrying a stick, which she waves around in front of her before stepping forward. What would you deduce from the situation? And what would you do?

We were made to understand that the woman must be blind, and hence, she was using the stick to try to feel her way across the road. We were told that the "right" thing to do would be to approach the woman, introduce yourself and help her cross the road.

The moral of the story was: Small actions can make a major difference in the lives of others.

I liked the idea of helping others. As a child, alongside my family, I'd actively participated in social activities like building village roads and furthering other causes. During the India war with China, our school had encouraged us to raise funds. For one week, we used to spend one hour every morning stopping pedestrians and cyclists on Bandar Road (since renamed Mahatma Gandhi Road), the national highway from Machilipatnam to Mumbai. Some people contributed one paisa, others five paisa. We raised Rs 168 for the Prime Minister's *Desa Rakshana Nidhi* (Nation Protection Fund).

I also remember being instructed to give a small bamboo basketful of rice to a woman who would pass by our home once a week. She always wore a *khadi* white saree and carried a metal can that was painted *Sarvodaya Patra*. I once asked her what she would do with the rice.

"Many people don't have food to eat," she said. "We'll distribute it among them."

When I was in college, I signed up with the National Service Scheme.

I got to visit many villages with the other volunteers and take part in grassroots community initiatives. The more I saw of the world, the more I realised how many people were deprived vis-à-vis the living conditions in my home. Working alongside like-minded youth for social causes was a great experience. We learned the value of a team.

My childhood dream had been to join the armed forces medical college. I was devastated when I didn't get the requisite score but I figured joining the National Cadet Corps (NCC) would at least help me savour military life. That experience was an eye opener.

The discipline in the NCC camp was unlike anything I had ever seen. I mean, my father was pretty strict with us. But at home, we were at least allowed to question our elders if we had a doubt to clarify. But the cadets "followed the leader" unquestioningly. No excuses were permissible, not even feeling down because of a monthly period! Once an order was issued, the cadets obeyed. They ate whatever was served, period.

My NCC exposure did a lot to enhance my feeling of nationalism and patriotism. Coming from a family of freedom fighters that meant a lot to me. It helped me understand the sort of feelings that had driven my family elders.

Until today I have great regard for the NCC. When my mother was appointed to chair the management committee of the *Zila Parishad* (District Council) Girls High School in Patamata Lanka, I requested her to introduce NCC in that school. She complied. In the seventies and eighties, it was a rarity for girl's schools to have NCC chapters. Since many professional colleges reserve seats for NCC cadets, those certificates helped many girls get ahead in life.

You learn a lot by living away from your hometown or your family. The first time most people live alone is when they travel for the sake of education, usually, a professional degree. At least, that's how things were for me. Relocating to Vishakhapatnam for a masters in social work at Andhra University marked the first time I lived away from home.

Life in a hostel showed me how privileged I had been at home. I learned to deal with limited resources such as water... with a lot of help from my roommate. I also learned how to manage time. I drew up study schedules and ended up spending most of my weekends in the library making notes.

Father had been very reluctant to send me to Vishakhapatnam because I had suffered from asthma since my childhood. In those days we had no inhalers or tablets for relief, just injections. Father didn't think I'd be able to manage myself. But I was adamant to go and mother backed me, so he relented.

What might have helped was the fact that father was a great one for education despite the fact that he had never had the privilege of being formally educated. It was he who encouraged me to apply for a fellowship to study at the Coady Institute in Canada after my daughter passed. He thought that getting back to books, my first love, would help me overcome the trauma of losing two loved ones that threatened to push me into a deep depression. He thought that I needed time away from our society where my "widow" status shadowed me wherever I went. I was feeling lost at the time and could hardly think straight. But

I got attracted to the idea of developing new professional skills, and so I went along with him.

I will always believe that the authorities in the Canadian consulate in New Delhi seconded father's thinking because of the way they reacted to my tragic story. They asked me about my personal life. I told them I had lost my husband and daughter in quick succession. They asked me to produce my husband's death certificate and my daughter's death certificate. Of course I wasn't carrying those documents so I got very stressed and started crying. But they didn't get upset with me. They just calmed me down and before I knew it, I had a student cum employment two-year multiple entry visa in hand. It was a big deal for that time.

I'm glad I took father's advice. My experience in Canada was an eye-opener from the word go.

Myself and Sharon Rebecca, another student, travelled together to Halifax. We were received by a team of lecturers on arrival. They escorted us to the campus where they showed us around and then handed us the keys to our room.

I was taken aback by the quality of the infrastructure and the campus ambience. My lodging was like a five-star hotel room. The choice of food in the cafeteria was unbelievable. My last degree had been from Andhra University and that was nowhere in comparison to the Coady Institute. All that was missing in Canada was lentils, rice and chicken gravy! At the weekends, students from India, Bangladesh and Sri Lankans would get together to cook such traditional favourites.

Everything about the environment at Coady was encouraging and student friendly. The style of teaching was participatory as opposed to the lectures I was used to. Professors would introduce a subject and then split us into groups of five to discuss the issue. Thereafter each group would present their learning. Essentially, we engaged in dialogues with the faculty and one another as opposed to the monologues I had seen in

India. We had amazing lecturers and guest lecturers. I quickly realised that the learning outcomes from such teaching methods would be far superior.

What also stood out about the Coady Institute was the global mix of students. We were a group of 68 students from 28 countries. Never before had I been exposed to people from so many diverse backgrounds. It deepened the learning and also gave me a multicultural exposure. Every now and then, the institute would organise cultural events and initiatives to promote community issues. I recollect one such occasion themed on the environment and climate change (and this was back in 1990!). While I was no stranger to activism, it was the first time that I saw an academic institution engage with the community. Blending academics with community activism made a lot of sense. It seemed a great way to introduce youth and talented minds to pressing issues.

At Coady, I learned that the origin of self-help groups could be traced to Canada. During the Second World War, women formed people's groups to empower themselves. I found this interesting because I had seen the difference that self-help groups could make in rural India.

I'd studied in a coeducation school and then with young women and men at Andhra University. I'd been married (and widowed) and had had (and lost) a daughter before I went to Canada. So I was by no means a novice at interacting with men. But during my time in the Coady Institute, I learned a valuable lesson about the equation between men and women in Canada, and that was, "In Canada, no truly means no."

It had so happened that I had gone to a post office to buy some postal stationary to write letters home. A young man at the counter said "Hi."

I wished him back.

Then he asked: "Where are you from?"

"India," I said.

"May we meet in the evening?"

Talk about being hit for six. I felt as though I had been raped. I left the stationary on the counter with the money and ran back to my room, sobbing.

Some hours later when my sobbing had still not abated I decided to seek help. I made my way to the faculty room, where I met with a female faculty member. She gave me a cup of tea and asked me why I was crying.

I narrated the incident.

"Oh!" she said. "I see. Well, if you didn't want to meet this man, all you had to say was 'no thank you.' There was no need to panic."

I stared at her unbelievingly through teary eyes. I couldn't believe the solution was so simple.

My respect for Canada went up several notches after hearing my faculty's advice. I told her that if I had been in India and a man had expressed an interest in me, he would have pestered me until he had had his way. He would never have taken no for an answer. That was why I had panicked.

Decades have passed since that episode but a woman's (or girl's) decline of interest still isn't taken seriously in India. It's sad. It makes me believe that there is something seriously wrong with our society, and that includes our education system.

During my time in Canada, I fell very sick. I experienced severe abdominal pain and vomiting, which was diagnosed as an intestinal obstruction. I was put on intravenous fluids for about 12 days. Thereafter I was advised to eat jelly while still admitted in hospital but my symptoms recurred. So I was operated on. After the surgery,

I got very depressed. The doctors and nurses were excellent, Sharon stayed back in the hospital the first night after my operation and my other batch-mates would take turns to visit me. But I missed having my family around to pamper me. Also, I felt very helpless. I would cry a lot because I was unable to walk. Then, an assistant doctor was asked to counsel me. He gave me numerous pep talks to motivate me, and handheld me as I started to walk. His support and encouraging words worked like a miracle. I realised the value of counselling patients undergoing long term treatment, something that I still feel is sorely missing in the Indian healthcare scenario. That experience in Canada reinforced my faith in the need to learn to live alone. You know what they say—we come into this world alone and we leave alone.

My last educational qualification came through in 2010—a certificate for successfully completing an executive development programme on private-public-partnerships at INSEAD, a world-renowned institute near Paris. I had applied for a fellowship for the course through the International HIV AIDS Alliance.

It was a remarkable opportunity for people from not-for-profit organisations to work with people from business, and understand how to imbibe skills from the business arena to improve the operations of not-for-profits and social enterprises. We were advised to look at things with the eye of a business person. That was an eye opener because I had always equated a business perspective with profit or money. At INSEAD, I learned to equate a business outlook with sustainability and using facts and data to justify the need for resources.

At INSEAD, the focus was on the deliverables. Where you sat in the classroom—at a table or on the floor—didn't matter. What counted was whether you could deliver. If you think of it, isn't ability all that matters?

Chapter 3

I don't think it's possible for a person with a rational bent of mind like me to fall in love at first sight.

It's not as if I am incapable of love. It's just that atheism has taken me very far from blind faith as well as from blind commitments. I am aware that my beliefs are starkly different from the majoritarian view. I am also certain that I don't want to push myself into an uncomfortable situation by committing my time, energy or myself, for that matter, without sufficient thought. You know what they say, act in haste, repent at leisure. Therefore, I think twice and then once again before taking any decision. Will it work in the long term, in view of my atheist mind-set?

By the time I was in university, I'd seen many inter-caste, inter-faith and inter-state marriages in my family and they were all successful. I attributed that to the fact that the atheist partner in all of those couples were in no hurry to get hitched. They stepped forward only after ensuring that they would be allowed to live on their own terms. They stepped forward only after reconciling their thinking with their prospective partners.'

So, when Vidyasagar Yerramsetty, a batch-mate in university, proposed to me when we were in our fourth semester, I told him that my single-minded goal was to prove myself to my parents. I wanted to show my parents that sending me to university had not been in vain. I wanted my parents to see me use education to give myself a leg up in life. Therefore, committing to him at the time was impossible.

It wasn't as if I disliked Vidyasagar.

We used to participate in academic group discussions and occasionally visit the library with other batch-mates. Vidyasagar knew me to be a very independent, hard-working, forward-looking young woman, with a no-nonsense outlook on life. He liked my attitude and the way I thought, he said.

But I hadn't figured out my feelings for him because as I said, getting together wasn't on my agenda at the time. I was sure that I wasn't in love with him but did I like him?

Maybe yes, subconsciously? Because, I didn't turn him down. Overtly, I hadn't sized him up because I wasn't thinking on those lines.

I told him about my priorities and made it clear that I didn't want to move forward until I had finished my masters. I suggested that he wait, if he was so inclined, and approach my parents thereafter.

I also made it clear to Vidyasagar that I wanted him to understand our belief system before asking for my hand. I wanted him to know where I was coming from. Because rationalism was firmly entrenched in me. It would always be the cornerstone of my life. My parents had taught me to be tolerant of other's views but I wanted to base my life on the same foundation that they had based theirs on.

"Marriage isn't a light decision, your views and values and beliefs must match mine, or, we must resolve those differences before we commit to each other," I said.

Love (or attraction) has its place but it isn't a replacement for the more rational process of thinking through your decisions. Unless you want to give up everything that makes you who you are, I call it "succumbing to your husband," you need to bridge your differences.

I was certain that I didn't want to stop being me. I'd developed an identity of my own in the 20-odd years of my life. I didn't see why I needed to drop that just because I was getting married. I reasoned: Vidyasagar had become a prospective because he had liked me. So why should I have changed the beliefs and values, the interests and tastes that defined me? I needed to be sure that Vidyasagar would let me be myself.

In my case, the salient difference between Vidyasagar and me was religion. But there are many other aspects that a couple could hold different views on. Dietary preferences, interests, backgrounds and more.

Vidyasagar was determined. He visited my parents after we had graduated and spent time understanding our atheist mind-set. He visited the atheist centre and read up on the concept. If he found it hard to digest our thinking, he never showed it. He himself was from a family of staunch Hindus. I was happy to let him continue practicing Hinduism as long as he placed no demand on me to practice the faith.

Vidyasagar would tell me that if atheism was behind my broadmindedness, if my rational approach to life had made me hardworking and confident, then, he was all for it. He really liked the atheist concept of not holding God responsible for the good and bad in your life. He showed himself to be a moderate in his views of God and religion.

"Rest assured that we will never clash on the grounds of religion," he said. "What matters is that we understand each other and support each other."

I trusted him.

Somewhere deep down, I felt he was the one. It helped that Vidyasagar held me in high esteem. That feeling was palpable in the way he treated me in private and in public.

It also helped that we had known each other for a good two years before he approached my parents. In that time, we, along with our other peers, discussed marriage and family life and got to know each other's views, strengths and weaknesses. We were both of the opinion that equality is essential for a successful, happy marriage. We both believed that marriage isn't a license for one spouse to dominate the other. Also, that marriage is an entry point for a healthy family. A healthy marriage paves the way for the family's wellbeing.

The ability to talk things through shows respect for each other. What sort of a future can you expect without respect? If you can't sit together and peacefully come to conclusions now, trust me, it will not work out. Run a mile.

Incidentally, in my work with a social organisation I have interacted with many couples coming in for counselling. It's saddening to hear them say that the relationship between a husband and wife isn't based on equality, and therefore, it's acceptable for the husband to dominate his wife. It also astounds me to hear people say that this inequality is rooted in religion.

My father seemed to like Vidyasagar but he insisted that his parents also be introduced to atheism. After all, a marriage isn't just a relationship between two individuals. A marriage brings together two families.

Father had reservations about staunch believers accepting a daughter-in-law from our background. He wanted to be sure that Vidyasagar's parents would accept me as I was. He knew that I wouldn't be able to change nor adjust in an orthodox Hindu household.

So both sets of parents met. Vidyasagar's father was a government employee while his mother was a home-maker. My father spelled out his expectations very clearly. I was to be allowed to continue to be an atheist. I was to be allowed to work after marriage. I wanted to sit for the Indian Administrative Service exam (at least attempt it once) for which I would need to spend the first year after getting married in Hyderabad where some family friends would put me up while I attended coaching classes.

Also, many of my relatives visited Vidyasagar's parents' home in Hanumakonda, where his father was posted at the time. The idea was for them to get to know more about us.

Despite the differences in our thinking, Vidyasagar's parents consented to the match. Behind the scenes, Vidyasagar had played his cards right. He had roped in his younger sister to speak well of me to their parents. He had made a big deal of the value I would bring to his life, both his personal life as well as his career, if we got married. Their father could never refuse his daughter anything so this was a smart move. What helped was the fact that Vidyasagar was looked on as a disciplined son, a son who would never do anything to bring dishonour to his family. To cut a long story short, their father agreed. His parents were only concerned about whether an educated daughter-in-law would agree to do household chores. These concerns were allayed after they met me and saw that I was adept in household work. My parents and my grandmother had always emphasised the need to be a multitasker. It wasn't enough to have a career. I had to turn to at home.

*

Father could well have afforded a wedding with all the bells and whistles but he sat me down and said: "Marriage isn't a celebration of money. I have enough money for a grand celebration but I want to be an example. Too many people who cannot afford a grand celebration take loans to get their children married and spend the rest of their lives repaying those debts. So the marriage becomes a burden for the family when actually, marriages should be a simple celebration. We must stand by what we believe in."

My parents had set a great example for me. I associated trust, simplicity, honesty and openness with marriage, and carried those very values into my own marriage.

In March 1978, Vidyasagar and I exchanged vegetable garlands made by my aunts. My grandmother and an uncle performed the ceremony in the presence of our family and friends. We sat on a makeshift dais. We wore *khadi*. The guests sat on large mats placed on the floor. Only home-made refreshments were served.

Our marriage was registered under the Special Marriages Act of 1954 a year later because I travelled to Hyderabad just a few days after our wedding. The Special Marriages Act requires a notice of marriage registration to be displayed for 90 days in the office of the registrar in the bride and groom's hometown. We had no time to comply with that formality so we postponed it.

In keeping with the spirit of the marriage, our reception in Hanumakunda (a town near Warangal where Vidyasagar's father was working at the time) was a simple dinner in a public garden, devoid of rituals, for which I was very grateful. His parents accepted me as I was without expecting me to wear the customary bridal accessories—jewellery and a *bindi*.

It mustn't have been easy for Vidyasagar's father because he was a state government employee with a huge circle, many of who may have had great expectations. All his colleagues were in attendance.

With Vidyasagar by my side, I gradually adjusted to married life. I didn't make it to the IAS, so, after that experience, I moved back to Vijayawada and started to work for Vasavya Mahila Mandali, the not-for-profit that my mother had founded. Vidyasagar left his job as a welfare officer with a textile mill in Warangal and joined me. He started a business—an electronics unit making TV-cum-radios. It was the first such manufacturing unit in Andhra Pradesh but then, Vidyasagar was pioneering in his thinking.

I enormously respected Vidyasagar for his thoughts and actions. We bonded very well sharing stuff with each other more like friends than as spouses. He would often say: "Only in the bedroom are we wife and husband, otherwise we are good friends."

One time, he wanted to start a new business. Vijayawada lies in district Krishna, an area very well known for its egg industry, which caters to both the domestic market as well as overseas markets. Vidyasagar wanted to start distributing egg trays. He asked me for my opinion. I loved the fact that he valued my suggestions. I also loved him for being transparent in his dealings. His finances were always in order. At every step in our marriage, he encouraged me to grow as a person.

Vidyasagar soon became a loving son to my parents. I knew him to be very concerned about his family but I found him to be equally concerned about my family. In fact, he would ask my father and mother for their opinion before taking any major business decision.

My father-in-law was very broad-minded and understanding. He had great regard for my knowledge, skills and ideas, and would often ask me for advice on investments. My mother-in-law was a rather fussy person especially in her eating habits. Nevertheless, I picked up a lot of cooking tips from her and was soon dishing up family favourites with some assistance from a helper. Both my parents-in-law celebrated my career successes.

I encouraged Vidyasagar's grandmothers (his grandfather had passed) to stay with us because I had grown up with my grandparents around and had always appreciated the presence of elders.

My equation with my in-laws wasn't always hunky-dory. The stark differences in my atheist beliefs and their Hindu beliefs stirred up emotions every now and then.

Soon after getting married, Vidyasagar and I had allocated a room in our home for his parents to pray in. They were happy with that. Then they said that they expected me to accompany them to the temples they visited.

"Okay," I said.

Visiting a temple wouldn't rock my boat. After all, hadn't I happily recited Christian prayers back in college? Isn't that what they call 'going with the flow'? I didn't think it made me small to visit a temple just as earlier in life, I hadn't thought it wrong to abide by my college code.

Next I learned that my mother-in-law would not enter the kitchen during her monthly period. She may have expected me to follow suit but I wasn't having any of that.

"I don't practice all those rituals," I said simply to Vidyasagar.

He was okay with that. So she had no choice but to accept the situation. If my mother-in-law was displeased with her son, I never got wind of it.

What I did feel hurt about was her reaction when I had an abortion. When I got home, my mother-in-law forbade me to enter the kitchen. If I thought she was saying so because I was feeling weak and needed rest, I was sadly mistaken. She had no such pious intention. She knew that I was still bleeding, so in her eyes, I was "dirty." And, it was below her dignity to serve me. She practically threw some food at me. There was nothing humane in her behaviour.

I knew where she was coming from so I never got into an argument with her. I just willed myself to understand her psychology. But I would be lying if I said that I wasn't hurt.

Another time Vidyasagar was travelling to Singapore to attend a conference on electronics. He was keen to take me along. My mother-in-law resisted. I felt bad but at the time, I told him: "It's okay, we can go another time."

Life is a trade-off, isn't it? We've got to take everyone with us, our family and close friends. When your thinking doesn't match, while you don't need to compromise on your principles, for the other things in life, sometimes you get your way, sometimes they get theirs. You can only enjoy family life when you understand the other person and the situation and adjust accordingly.

Vidyasagar did his best to make up for many such hurtful moments. Looking back, I realise that I was never very ambitious. All I wanted was an understanding husband and a peaceful family life. Beyond doubt I had the best husband in Vidyasagar. We simply never got into an argument. He would sort out every difference of opinion very peacefully.

Vidyasagar's attitude and support encouraged me to do whatever I could to care for my in-laws and to fully back him when he wanted to do something for his family. One time when my sister-in-law was bedridden because of severe arthritis, we took it upon ourselves to care for her until she had fully recovered, and resettle her and her children near our home.

I looked forward to the opportunity to nurture a new life as lovingly as I had been brought up. I wanted my children to be responsible citizens. I wanted to see the smile on their faces. I wanted to revel in their successes. I wanted to hold their hand in their difficult moments. I wanted them to hold my hand when I was down. I wanted them to become the sort of person everyone feels proud to know, the sort of person who gives back rather than takes from society. And, I wanted to bring up my children with Vidyasagar, a man who I loved dearly.

Vidyasagar and I had a daughter in October 1981. She was born on Durga-ashtami (like me). My parents-in-law were kind enough to not insist on giving her a Hindu name. We named her Swetcha (meaning 'freedom') in keeping with our family custom of naming children after a current event. The previous month, my maternal uncle Lavanam had attended a conference for free thinkers. We looked upon the atheist movement as a movement towards freedom.

My in-laws welcomed Swetcha believing that a baby girl is symbolic of Goddess Laxmi, the goddess of wealth. They were keen to celebrate her birth but we had to postpone any occasion for when she was a few months old. Swetcha was a very tiny, sick baby and needed a lot of care in her first few months. She got all of that as well as a lot of love and pampering as a baby from her parents as well as from her grandparents. In fact, my father-in-law used to offer to look after Swetcha.

Vidyasagar and I had discussed having a family and I had made it clear that I wanted to bring up my children as atheists. So, like me, Swetcha grew up imbibing atheist concepts. Like me, she was taught to be tolerant of other faiths. In fact, she had far more opportunities than me to practice tolerance. I grew up amongst atheists at home. But Swetcha had one set of orthodox Hindu grandparents. Whenever my mother-in-law wanted her to take part in a religious function, she complied even though she had no faith in what was happening. I was proud of her. As for Vidyasagar. Sadly, he wasn't around. We lost him very early.

Chapter 4

On October 30, 1987, Vidyasagar, Swetcha and I were travelling in a van from Vijayawada to Hyderabad. We were on our way to attend an event organised by my mother. Vidyasagar was driving. Swetcha and I were sitting in the front passenger seat. My younger sister Deeksha and a support person were sitting at the back.

About 50 kilometres away from Hyderabad, all of a sudden, a pedestrian crossed the road. Vidyasagar swerved to avoid hitting the man causing our vehicle to skid off the highway and roll into a ditch. The front part of the van bore the brunt of the crash. It broke into two. All the doors got jammed. Deeksha had the presence of mind to let herself out of the car and help us out. That is, help Swetcha, me and the support person. We weren't too badly injured but Vidyasagar appeared to be unconscious with severe steering wheel injuries. This was decades before safety air bags were fitted in cars.

By then a few villagers had gathered and with their help, Deeksha, who is a doctor, managed to get Vidyasagar out of the van and lay him on the ground. Then she started to give him first aid. She instructed me to go to the highway and flag a vehicle to help us take him to a hospital.

Myself, our assistant and Swetcha did as she had said. To no avail. Until about an hour had passed, when two young men stopped their car and agreed to help us. We sat on the back seat with Vidyasagar lying on our laps. He was still alive. Swetcha sat with the other passenger in the front. We travelled the remaining distance to Dilshuknagar in the outskirts of Hyderabad where my sister-in-law's brother Shanti Babu lived. He was a doctor.

Shanti Babu suggested that he and Deeksha would take Vidyasagar to Osmania Hospital, and I should stay back with his wife Dr Sudha. I let them go but there was no way I was staying back. I requested Dr Sudha to find someone to accompany me to the hospital. She sent me with their hospital nurse. We travelled in an auto rickshaw.

I will never forget the moment I entered the casualty. Deeksha came up to me and gave me a big hug. Then she said: "Brother-in-law is no more."

Behind her, I saw his body lying inert. A white cloth had been draped over it.

I didn't know how to react. I didn't know whether to burst into tears or what.

I was drawn to the reaction of those around me. My daughter didn't understand what was going on. She kept asking: "Where is daddy?"

Hearing her, I felt like crying but I held myself together.

Mother reached the hospital soon after and burst into tears. Since she was a cardiac patient, I tried to calm her down but she wouldn't stop crying.

We filed a police complaint to start the formalities of registering the death. The commissioner of police was a gem. He processed the case instantly. I can never forget his brotherly affection. The way he asked a female constable to care for Swetcha, and even buy her an ice-cream while the paperwork was being done. And the speed at which he arranged for us to transfer the body to Vijayawada.

The Governor of the state Kumudben Joshi called mother to condole Vidyasagar's death. She made a special request to the hospital to quickly complete the formalities.

Back in Vijayawada, father's reaction was similar to mother's. In fact, he mourned Vidyasagar's demise for many, many years. He had always been a hot-headed man. But after Vidyasagar passed, father became very quiet, very calm. I always felt as if something within him died with that episode.

I was stunned to see how many people came to pay their last respects to Vidyasagar. I expected my extended family to attend but there were also people from the local community and from other parts of the state. Vidyasagar was so well known.

The day after Vidyasagar died, there was chaos at home. My in-laws insisted on performing traditional rituals. I was in my own space dealing with my sorrow so I didn't intervene. I had lost the person I loved the most. What did I care about what was going on? I wanted to be left alone. But that was impossible.

My mother-in-law and other women (I must underline women) in the family descended on me with a volley of do's and don'ts. For instance, I was told not to show my face in the morning, just the opposite to when Vidyasagar had been alive and my in-laws wanted me to get up early and get on with the housework. Obviously, when you work you are seen. You can't hide yourself.

Suddenly, in the space of a day, my presence had become a bad omen.

My in-laws' behaviour starkly contrasted with the way widows were treated in my family. I had never seen a widow discriminated against, or looked down upon in any way. Widows in my family had the same rights as anyone else. They remarried if they wanted.

At the outset, I did whatever my in-laws told me to do, said whatever they told me to say. My mind had gone blank. I felt rudderless, like a boat drifting in the sea. I felt directionless, like I didn't know what to do with myself.

Why had my best friend's time to go come so early?

I didn't want to just hold him in my heart. I wanted him by my side to guide me and hold my hand. But he had moved on.

Why?

We were so young. Our life together had got off to a flying start. Swetcha was only four years old. Vidyasagar's career was just taking off. Even the Chief Minister of the state at the time (NT Rama Rao) had lauded him for his entrepreneurial spirit.

Vidyasagar's passing was the start of a slide.

My in-laws were shattered... obviously, who wouldn't be, at the loss of a son? Or a husband, for that matter. I was shattered too. But their pain turned into anger and abuse, all of which was directed on me.

In their mind, I was the cause for their son's premature death. I had brought misfortunate on their son, on their family, and yes, on myself too.

On the third day after Vidyasagar died, I asked my sister Rashmi to accompany me to the Veeramachaneni Paddayya Siddhartha Public School for Swetcha's admission. At the time, Swetcha was a student of the Takshasila Public School, a residential school in Hyderabad. Vidyasagar and I had admitted her there because I had been hard pressed for time in the last couple of years. Vidyasagar's sister had fallen severely ill and bedridden in 1984, and the task of caring for her and her three children aged one to seven years had fallen on me. Additionally, I had household responsibilities including hosting a stream of relatives who visited my sister-in-law. Vidyasagar and I had felt that Swetcha would be better off in a residential school. It had been painful to leave her at that young age but it had seemed the best choice.

With Vidyasagar having gone, I wanted to keep Swetcha with me. In any case my sister-in-law, having recuperated, had moved to her own home earlier in 1987.

The Veeramachaneni Paddayya Siddhartha Public School authorities had asked Swetcha to sit for an entrance test after which the admission process was completed.

When I returned, my mother-in-law approached me in great anger and asked: "How dare you go out the third day after your husband has died? Don't you know that you're a widow? You can't step out until so-and-so ritual has been performed."

For the first time in my life I was addressed as a widow.

I didn't tell my mother-in-law that I was willing myself to appear as normal as possible for Swetcha's sake.

Swetcha only understood the meaning of absent and present. She felt the absence of a parent. At the age of four, she couldn't understand death. It's very challenging to explain death to a child.

I had told her that her father had gone overseas. I regretted lying to her but I didn't know how else to handle the situation. She would keep asking me when her father would return from overseas. I had no proper answer for her. I'd try to avoid her questions or else just say "Soon."

My mother-in-law worsened matters by placing a garlanded photograph of Vidyasagar on a mantelpiece with a small light next to it. Swetcha would cry bitterly every time she passed it. I wanted to request my mother-in-law to remove it because of the way it was affecting Swetcha but I felt it would be of no use.

I would try to mollify Swetcha but seeing that photograph day in and day out didn't help her nor me. I wanted to remember Vidyasagar as a living legend.

About a fortnight after Vidyasagar's death, my eldest sister Rashmi accompanied me to the office of the revenue collector to apply for a family member's certificate.

He said: "Although your marriage is registered, we must conduct a *panchnama* (a public inquiry) before issuing the family member's certificate."

I pointed out that our marriage had been registered under the Special Marriage Act and that I had attached all the supporting documents. But he didn't agree.

"Your husband could have had another wife after you," the tehsildar said.

What sort of comment was that? I realised that the man was enjoying the opportunity to shame me. I was soon to realise the minimal value placed on a registered marriage.

Some representatives of the revenue collector's office visited my neighbourhood and asked a few random people if I had been Vidyasagar's wife until his last breath?

In the years since, I have heard many other widows say that they have experienced similar shaming instances.

I can understand the need for formalities to be completed but why does the widow have to be shamed in the process? Why can't our systems be more sensitive? I am convinced that this rot arises from religious beliefs that endorse a negative perception of widows. Those same beliefs led my in-laws to abuse me and curse me after Vidyasagar died.

I couldn't understand their thinking nor their behaviour. When their behaviour became unbearable, I told my parents about the situation. It was the natural thing to do. They had been my pillars of support after Vidyasagar's death. They would visit me every day, spend time with me and play with Swetcha. The rest of my family also stood by me.

My parents and an uncle approached my in-laws several times to discuss the situation. Their interaction was always amicable but nothing came of it.

After Vidyasagar's death I had continued to welcome my in-laws to my home believing that they were family. They would stay with me off and on since my father-in-law was still working and posted out of Vijayawada. What was strange was that they started to lock their room in my home whenever they left.

I let out a portion of my home. Swetcha and I depended on the rent to get by. Those were very difficult days. I was compelled to sell my silver to run the household.

My home was constructed on land my father had gifted to me when I was 21. On the front side of the property, we had constructed a building to let out for commercial activities. On the back side, we had a second building which housed our residence on the ground floor. We had used the first floor used for Vidyasagar's electronic manufacturing unit and office. Vidyasagar, my father and my father-in-law had all contributed to the cost of construction. After his death, I willed myself to continue his business. It was an emotional decision. A poor decision because I lacked the skills to do so. Much later I wound up the business.

But to come back to the time soon after Vidyasagar's death, my in-laws tried to dissuade my tenants from staying with me. When I told my mother what was going on, she approached my tenants and asked them to consider me to be their sister, not their landlady.

It's very important for women to own their family property. If my home had been in my husband's name, I am certain that my in-laws would have done their best to throw me out. As things turned out, my property turned out to be my greatest security. It became a source of income.

Vidyasagar had pledged my house to the state financial corporation against a loan for his manufacturing unit. My parents helped me sort out that matter by taking full responsibility for the loan. They helped me to start a fertiliser distributorship, which I ran for about a decade at the end of which I had earned enough money to clear all of Vidyasagar's debts. I have no words to express my gratitude to my parents.

It wasn't just my in-laws who had a problem with me. A few months after losing Vidyasagar, I realised that society was bypassing me for auspicious events. In India, the widely prevailing belief is that widows bring misfortune and so, they should be confined at home.

One day, my sister Deeksha asked me to accompany her for so-and-so's wedding. I was taken by surprise because I hadn't received an invitation card. Deeksha said I must have been missed in error. So I accompanied Deeksha and her husband Meher to the marriage.

When I was blessing the newly married couple, I heard the other women on the dais grumbling about my presence.

"How dare she bless the couple when her husband died just three months ago. It's inauspicious for us. Why isn't she at home?"

Interestingly, I didn't hear any man on the dais complain. In time, I realised that women talk the most about other women. Women are the least likely to show concern for a disadvantaged woman. Not that men don't hassle widows.

After I was widowed, I heard comments from so many quarters that I gradually grew more aloof. I realised that not only did society stigmatise me but it pushed me into stigmatising myself. I preferred to avoid social gatherings. I grew isolated. Wasn't that what society wanted of me?

I was a member of the Inner Wheel Club of Vijayawada. Back in 1987 only women whose husband was a member of the Rotary Club could become members of the Inner Wheel Club. Now the systems have changed. Even women who are unmarried or those whose husband is not a Rotarian can join the Inner Wheel.

Anyway, a few months after Vidyasagar passed some representatives of the Inner Wheel Club visited me and told me that I had to resign from the club. I asked them why. They pointed out that my husband had died.

"Oh!" I thought. "So I have ceased to exist too."

What a strange system. When women most need support, they are asked to get out. Instead of helping, even a so-called "prestigious" club rubbed salt into the wounds of a widow. I realised that the respect that people showed me while Vidyasagar was alive was just because of his status.

I resigned from the Inner Wheel. In the ensuing months, a couple of other women who were members were also asked to resign after losing their husband.

My family didn't want me to withdraw into a shell but I was hurt, terribly hurt. Perhaps to vent that pain, I felt the need to rebel against societal attitudes and customs that didn't allow a widow to heal and move on.

I used to wonder if wearing a *bindi* was such a big deal? Why is a *bindi* associated with the wearer's marital status?

I recollected that my grandfather had asked his brother's bride, a widow, to wear a *bindi*. He was trying to change the system. I had never worn a *bindi* during my married life but to make a stand, I started to wear a *bindi* and flowers in my hair after I was widowed. It is up to us to change the system.

Would you invite a widow to a family event? Would you ask a widow to perform a ceremony? Would you blame her for her widowhood? Would you let her widowhood take precedence over herself?

A woman who married at 19 and was widowed at 21 once came to us at Vasavya Mahila Mandali. She sat in front of us with a baby on her lap. She wanted to build a life for herself. Today, she is an entrepreneur.

Some decades ago, widowhood was a good enough reason to banish a woman. To expect her to stop caring for her appearance. To think of a single woman (unmarried or widowed) as "available." Myself and scores of unmarried women and widows have had men hit on them with bad intentions.

I expect youth to take society away from these regressive discriminatory practices.

*

In the first week of September 1989, Swetcha took ill. She was in the third grade at the time. We consulted a general practitioner who diagnosed her fever as a viral flu, and prescribed a five-day course of medicine. She got better but she still felt very weak. So the doctor suggested that she rest at home for a week. On the ensuing weekend, I gave her a good bath and washed her beautiful, curly hair. I was feeling under the weather so I took a nap after bathing her. Later that evening, it was the seventeenth of September, a Sunday, she came to me saying that she wasn't feeling well. She had a very high fever. I rushed her to my uncle's place because no hospital was open, only to find that he was out with his wife. My grandmother who lived next door suggested to sponge down Swetcha with water cooled with ice cubes and give her an anti-pyretic syrup. I did that until my uncle was available, and he confirmed that we had done the right thing. He also suggested giving her blood for a culture test the next morning. We did so and were asked to pick up the report after three days.

In the interim, Swetcha continued to suffer a high fever despite all our efforts. When I went to pick up the report, they told me that they couldn't do the test as the blood hadn't been taken properly. They asked me to bring Swetcha the next morning.

I felt very bad. I couldn't understand their negligence. Surely they could have intimated us if the blood test couldn't be performed?

That same evening, Swetcha started to throw up blood. We shifted her to my uncle's nursing home where we kept her in the operation theatre because that was the only room with air-conditioning. More than 10 doctors attended to her, two from the nursing home and eight more specialists who had been specially called in.

What made matters worse was that even slight bleeding from an injection site wouldn't abate. We were advised to identify volunteers who could donate 'O'-negative blood, her blood group. My uncle stepped forward to donate blood as did an employee of mine. We reached out to every contact we had to collect sufficient blood. All this continued overnight.

Doctors told us that they could consider shifting Swetcha to the All India Institute of Medical Sciences in New Delhi, the country's premier medical institution, only after her vomiting stopped. My mother was a member of parliament so they thought she would have contacts in that premier medical institution. They also put her on intravenous fluids.

Early the next morning they stopped the fluids and the transfusions. Suddenly, she had a cardiac arrest. They did whatever they could. She was put on oxygen but they couldn't revive her.

Swetcha had always wanted to donate her eyes. I told my maternal uncle that I wanted to fulfil her wish. That decision upset my in-laws but my family stood by me.

I was in a very bad mental state after Swetcha's death. Seeing my suffering, my parents suggested that I apply for further studies at the Coady Institute in Canada. Father thought that I needed time away from our society where my "widow" status shadowed me wherever I went, on top of which, I was hurting from the loss of my only child.

I could hardly think straight. But I got attracted to the idea of developing new professional skills, and so I went along with father's idea.

Swetcha was my only link with my in-laws. After I left India for Canada, they visited my home. Who know what they had in mind? But my father and other family members stepped in to sort matters out. Father told them to clear out their possessions once and for all. In fact, my father arranged a lorry for their stuff. They cleaned out all the furniture and soft furnishings. Everything except what was in my bedroom.

*

The possibility of remarrying first came up in Canada during my time at the Coady Institute. A couple of people proposed to me. I was simply not in that space at the time but they were quite insistent. Even after I declined and returned to India, they would write to me and express their interest.

About a year after I returned, I grew very close to a family friend and felt that we would marry. But he cheated me. All the time we were interacting, he was looking for a girl to marry.

I was taken aback and so were my parents. They wanted me to have nothing to do with him. Still, I attended his wedding.

My parents wanted me to remarry. They felt that I was very young.

"You're only in your thirties," they would say.

All my sisters were well settled and I guess they felt that I stood out.

On the one hand, I wasn't sure what to do. I knew I was still young but I didn't have feelings for anyone. Getting together with someone new held the possibility of being hurt again. I couldn't bear that. On the other hand, I thought perhaps I should remarry to please my parents.

My parents started to look around for a suitable match. They also advertised in the matrimonial column of our local newspaper.

One response to their ad came from a man named Kesavarao who said that he was an executive engineer who had lost his wife. We all thought that it made sense to consider a widower for me.

We asked a relation to do a background check. Only thereafter was I introduced to Kesavarao and he was invited to meet my father.

Kesavarao told my father that his parents objected to him marrying a widow but he was committed to doing so. Hearing that, my father asked a relative to visit his elder brother to ascertain his views on our marriage. He had said that he had no problem with his brother marrying me.

Kesavarao told me that he was very religious and a follower of Shirdi Sai Baba (a saint in India). I told him about atheism but left it at that. I no longer had the energy and enthusiasm I had had at the time I married Vidyasagar to go through reconciling the differences in our beliefs.

Kesavarao didn't ask me much about my past. Nor did he express any surprise about the fact that I wasn't dressed like a widow. I used to wear light jewellery and a *bindi*. I thought he might have attributed my dress sense to our modern outlook.

After having lost the two people I was closest to in my life, I didn't want to get emotionally attached again. I still hurt from my past losses. Yes, I was getting married again but it was more to please my parents. I was very casual about the whole thing.

I told Kesavarao about Swetcha. I also told him that I had had a hysterectomy after my first husband had passed because I had suffered from gynaecological issues. So, I wouldn't be able to have any more children. He didn't appear to be bothered by that submission.

He told me that he had a bachelors' degree in commerce and his own real estate business. The difference between what he had advertised himself to be and what he actually was, was troubling but I chose to overlook it because he told me that he had bluffed to improve his prospects.

"All I want is a peaceful life," I told my parents, to justify my stance. "I'm not looking for a life of luxury."

Still, I made it clear to Kesavarao that I expected honesty going forward.

We had a small ceremony in 2001 wherein we exchanged garlands followed by a small reception attended only by my very close relatives. We understood that his parents would not attend but we had expected his elder brother and sister-in-law to attend.

Kesavarao didn't take me home after our marriage ostensibly because of his parents' views.

Instead, about 10 days after our marriage, he called me to Hyderabad. We checked into a hotel. That first night, he asked me all sorts of questions about the bangles I was wearing.

"What do they weigh?"

He continuously pestered me to tell him the weight of the bangle. I told him I couldn't remember. But he kept asking. He said strange things like: "They are very heavy bangles."

I couldn't understand the motive behind his questions.

Later when we shifted into a house, he didn't shell out any money for the house rent or any bills. I was running the household on my income.

Before we had gotten married he had told us that he had a car. But he didn't have a car, just a two-wheeler.

I didn't mind the step down and never refused to travel by his two-wheeler. I valued simplicity as well as a peaceful household. But I wasn't comfortable with his lies.

This situation continued for about a year before I sat him down and asked him point blank why he wasn't contributing to the household.

"You had said that you had business contracts... so why aren't you meeting any household expenses?" I asked.

He told me that he had debts of about INR 7–8 million to settle.

I refused to take that for an answer. I asked him for details of all of his debts, the capital amounts, the interest rates and so on. I also asked him to prioritise those outstanding debts. I would repeatedly get very annoyed because he had no sense of money. I would meticulously plan our finances and he would mess it up by withdrawing money without asking me.

Another time I set aside some money to buy a car. When it came to paying for the insurance, I found that my account had been cleaned out. He had withdrawn everything using my ATM card.

He sold about 200 grams of gold that I had kept in our home locker. We had to shift to a smaller house in Hyderabad because he wasn't earning.

By then I was also very concerned about the fact that he had continuously resisted getting our marriage registered under the Special Marriage Act (it took me three years to get that done).

Should that have set alarm bells ringing?

I started to feel depressed. I'd ask myself:

What is this life?

Why did I get married?

Is there any meaning in our marriage?

Kesavarao started to vanish for a few days at a time. He would return home late at night. He would lie to me. He would do his own thing. When I questioned him, sometimes, he would answer calmly and sometimes, he would react.

In 2003, my brother visited Hyderabad and told us that a large construction project was coming up in Vijayawada, which would create lucrative opportunities for Kesavarao.

My brother approached the developers on behalf of a firm in which both he and Kesavarao were partners. They were awarded a contract after a lot of negotiation. We relocated to Vijayawada and stayed in our own home.

Kesavarao did well but he still didn't contribute to our household expenses. Also, he would move away from me to receive phone calls at home. When I questioned him, he would throw a tantrum. He'd break a chair or the TV or his mobile and shout loudly. His actions seemed aimed at intimidating me.

Gradually all of this increased. He never laid a hand on me but in some ways his actions were worse than that because he created a negative environment at home in which anything could have happened.

I started to mistrust him. He took a bank loan in my name to buy land in Hyderabad. He ignored me when I asked for the title deed but I kept pestering him. When he finally produced the documents, I saw that the land was in his name. I didn't recognise the address he had provided. I kept the document in my locker. That was of no use. He found the key I had hidden away and took them away.

He made me pay for two new SUVs. We applied for a four-wheeler driving licence for him. I got to know that he wasn't a graduate, he was only a matriculate. On hindsight, I realise that I should have walked out then. Instead, I tolerated him and his ways because I wanted my marriage to be successful. I knew that it meant a lot to my parents that I was married and I wanted them to be happy.

Instead of fretting I applied my energy to trying to figure out why he repeatedly lied to me. What was behind his obnoxious behaviour? Where did he go every now and then?

I found out that he was not a widower as he had said. He was a much married man with two young children from his first wife.

I was shocked. I wanted to get out of the marriage immediately.

When I approached Kesavarao, he said that as I had no children, he had thought that I would accept his two after some time. I thought that that was unfair. He hadn't come clean from the start.

He had cheated me. He had seen me as a good catch because I was financially sound. Financial independence is important for a woman but it makes her vulnerable to being misused by men almost just as much as being penniless does.

In 2007, I finally told my parents what was going on in my personal life. My father was on his deathbed at the time. But my mother and other family members stood by me and suggested that I register for a doctoral programme to apply my energy to something constructive and release some stress.

Our situation at home was very unpleasant. If I asked him about our relationship, he would snap. If I suggested that we go out for a drive, he would drive rashly, so rashly that I thought he would hit an electric pole. "I want you to die," he'd say.

Twice, he threw burning camphor from his prayer tray at me and both times my saree caught fire. So much for worship. Once again in my life, I wondered what use it was to acknowledge God when your actions are so far removed from Godliness.

Once I had enough evidence to prove in court that he was already married when he had supposedly married me, I proposed that we apply for a mutual divorce. I told him that he had not only cheated me but also his wife and children.

Deeksha asked Kesavarao to settle his debts and seconded my call for a mutual divorce. Mother called in the best lawyers while Deeksha tracked the case. My family tried to sort out the matter as amicably as possible.

At every step of the way, I felt that my family had my back, and that meant the world to me. My family was my backbone. It gave me the confidence to call out Kesavarao for his wrongs and detach myself from him.

After our divorce came through in 2009, my family ensured that Kesavarao cleared out his belongings from my home.

I had already experienced what it was like to be a widow. After our divorce came through, I had a whole lot of new experiences, mostly unpleasant.

The 'divorcee' tag weighs heavy on the wearer. Divorcees are an even lower cadre than widows. We're shunned socially, so much so that even I used to hesitate to say that I was single. I was scared of the social repercussions.

I used to wonder if I would be blamed for my status? Also, I didn't want to invite unwanted male attention. As a widow, I had already been the recipient of unwanted sexual advances. Being attached to a man is a sort of a safety net for a woman. It took me all of nine years to make peace with my status. I willed myself to come out as a divorcee only by the faith that it might help other women.

I had nothing to do with Kesavarao after our divorce. But in 2012, I received a call from him. He said that he had been hospitalised and expressed the wish to see me one last time. I didn't trust him so I didn't respond affirmatively. He called me again. I asked him what the matter was. He said he was dying of leukaemia. He was admitted in Apollo Hospitals, Hyderabad.

I have always believed that last wishes should be fulfilled, even those of our enemies. I also believe in not having any enemies, and especially not considering a former husband an enemy. So I travelled to Hyderabad to see him. I didn't let him know beforehand because in the back of my mind, I harboured doubts.

It was true. He was admitted for leukaemia. He had had many rounds of chemotherapy. He was all skin and bones.

Did I feel upset?

He gave me no chance. I had hardly arrived when he started to badger me for money. "Give me some money, give me 7 million rupees, my treatment may cost even 10 million rupees."

It felt like yesterday once more.

He hadn't changed at all. He still wanted to live on others.

I told him that I had only rupees two hundred thousand in a fixed deposit, which I was willing to contribute to the cost of his treatment. "Don't consider it a loan," I said. "It's a contribution."

He started to abuse me and blame me as if I was the cause of his cancer. He called me a cheater. He didn't realise that I owed him nothing. And that he had given me nothing but sorrow.

Chapter 5

Growing up, there was never a doubt in my mind about the fact that I would have to work as an adult to earn a living.

Father would make it a point to take my siblings and me to his business premises from a very young age, where he would introduce us to the basics of running a business. He made it clear that women were meant to be financially independent, never dependent on their father or husband.

"To be financially independent you have to work," he'd say.

My maternal grandmother was a living, exemplary example of a woman, widowed early in life, who successfully brought up four children by her sheer strength of character and ability to turn to. She lost no opportunity to earn money, selling buttermilk, weaving cloth and even selling cow dung cakes to supplement her meagre family income. She drilled the importance of financial independence in my siblings and me. So we grew up with the understanding that a work culture was normal. Every individual had to work to be financially independent.

Father wanted us to learn how to make as well as manage money. He explained the usefulness of life insurance policies and legitimate chit funds. He opened a bank account for each of us when we turned 18. He'd give us one hundred rupees and ask us to track where we spent it. And he was a great one for saving. "You have to save one-fourth of your salary, no matter how much you earn," he'd say.

Father was a robust financial manager. He had no degree in finance but his common sense more than made up for his lack of formal education.

After I got married my husband and I thought of constructing a small home on a plot that father had gifted me. Father turned around and said, "Don't spend all your money on building a house. A house will not yield you any income. Build a small shopping complex and a small house behind it. A small, liveable place is enough."

So that was what my husband and I did, and after I was widowed that asset stood me in good stead. I had the rental income from the complex to rely on and that ensured that my in-laws treated me well.

*

To come back to my career, I got my master's degree around the middle of 1977. Soon after I was inundated with telegrams from reputed companies such as Parry's (a sugar brand) and ITC (a company with a presence across verticals) offering me a job as a labour officer or personnel officer. I didn't jump on any offer as around then, I was preoccupied with the arrangements for my brother's wedding and my own engagement.

That November Andhra Pradesh was struck by a devastating tropical cyclone and storm surge that officially killed 10,000. Unofficially the death count was at least five times higher. About 3.4 million people lost their homes and livelihoods.

I was moved by the enormity of the suffering and offered my service to the Arthik Samata Mandal (Association for Economic Equality), an organisation providing relief to some of the worst affected communities on the island of Diviseema.

A bout of abdominal pain sent me back home where I was diagnosed with appendicitis. I had to set aside my aspiration to help people for a few months. But by March 1978, I was back on the job, this time, professionally as my uncle offered me a formal position with the Arthik Samata Mandal. My monthly salary was two thousand five hundred rupees. That marked the start of my career in the social development sector, a sector I have stuck to all my life.

The idea of joining a corporation didn't appeal to me. I was taken up by the idea of helping people and transforming lives. My mind had been irrevocably shaped by my childhood exposure.

Mother would make it a point to explain the working of small Mahila Mandals (women's groups) and tell us how they made a difference to the lives of socio-economically less privileged women. She also told us about Zila Parishads (district councils), which offered schemes for the development of villages.

Mother became a member of the Andhra Pradesh State Advisory Board while I was still studying. She encouraged me to help small not-for-profit organisations by writing out their grant proposals. To help us realise the value of the education we were being given, she would tell us that they lacked the skills to fill out proposals.

When father started a cooperative society for lorry owners, he emphasised the power of a group in protecting the right of individuals. "We're voiceless as individuals," he'd say. "But together we can demand our rights from the government."

Father also shared nuggets on how to run a co-operative society.

Father and mother both lay great emphasis on participating in community development activities such as road laying. Their attitude instilled a strong sense of social responsibility in their children.

My parents were always sought after by the community for their suggestions on various matters. Seeing them share their thoughts so freely made me realise the need to give back wherever and however possible.

Grandfather played a huge role in emboldening me to speak up for those who cannot express themselves out of fear or a lack of confidence or ability to do so. Grandfather and my maternal uncle also showed me the importance of activism. The freedom movement was a campaign. They would tell me, "Now we are free but what about alleviating poverty?"

They were strongly against the ostentatious display of wealth, the wastage of resources and the pomp of government. They taught me to value simplicity, and to ensure that every rupee contributed for a social cause was stretched as far as possible.

Their inspiration has lasted a lifetime. Until today, I cannot turn away from a have-not, a woman in need, the underdog. Until today, I believe I chose well for myself. I wouldn't have opted for any other career.

I worked with the Arthik Samata Mandal through to 1980. During those years, I interacted with donors of their relief programmes and child care programmes. I also interacted with the beneficiaries of these programmes, and that was so rewarding. The greatest contentment for me is to bring a smile to the face of a person who is suffering.

I took a two-year break from work thereafter to care for my new born. In 1982, I joined Vasavya Mahila Mandali, a women's led not-for-profit working for women. My first position was programme coordinator. Thereafter, I became the director of programmes, then technical support manager and in 2018, president of the organisation.

Soon after I started to work I realised that my academic degree had given me a sound understanding of certain social theories but very little understanding of what happened on the ground. When you venture out you learn things that you are never taught in a classroom.

Academic courses also tend to be outdated, according to me.

During my journey with Vasavya Mahila Mandali, I've learned a lot about the real economic, social and legal issues women face. I have developed skills related to advocacy, project monitoring and evaluation, communication and collaboration, storytelling, networking, reporting and digitalisation.

I've also worked with corporations, providing technical support on areas such as training employees, establishing committees to prevent and deal with sexual harassment at the workplace, and implementing corporate social responsibility.

The general view is that the not-for-profit sector doesn't attract the most talented people because it doesn't need the same level of skills that a corporation does. I beg to differ. My lifetime's experience in the not-for-profit sector and my work with corporations have shown me that the not-for-profit sector demands a different set of skills but one which is no less complex than what is applied in for-profit organisations.

There's a lot that a person engaged in the not-for-profit sector can learn from a corporation just the same as those in for-profit organisations can learn a lot from the non-governmental sector.

The perspective that the not-for-profit sector is soft on skills may come from the lack of professionalism in many such organisations. It's why I have always prioritised updating my skills. I have travelled a lot both within India and overseas to attend training events and conferences where I have presented papers. I am passionate about documenting work and putting together case studies that showcase grassroots change and the impact of societal research. The right documentation helps to build credibility for an organisation.

As a leader in the non-governmental sector, my focus has been to walk the talk. To uphold what you claim to stand for. And, to do whatever you claim to be your mandate. Walking your talk is vital to beget respect. And in the not-for-profit sector, respect is critical to attract finance. I've also learned a hands on approach to lead a team through a crisis. Taking a back seat is not the sign of a leader.

It is a fact that salaries in the social sector are lower than in the for-profit sector. That's a big put off for many potential aspirants, and pushes them to corporate life. You have to weigh the pros and cons of every opportunity to figure out what will work for you. I was lucky to have an alternate source of income (rental income) aside my job with Vasavya Mahila Mandali. Having a separate stream of income ensured that I was always financially comfortable.

*

My atheist upbringing has strongly impacted my work ethic. I don't believe misfortunate is anyone's fate. I don't believe you carry forward positive or negative karma. Misfortunate is just a negative situation, according to me. I believe we (and not a divine power) have the power to change situations. So when I meet women who have suffered in life, I wipe their tears and tell them to make the most of the opportunity to change their lives. I've always seen every personal crisis as an opportunity, and encourage others to do likewise.

When you face a downturn in your career or a financial crisis in life, consider upgrading your skills, particularly your employable skills, and your knowledge.

I once met a woman who was married at 14 years when she was in standard nine. She hadn't wanted to marry so young. She had wanted to study to be a nurse. By the age of 18 she had had two children. Her husband was lethargic and epileptic so the task of running the household fell on her. She started to work as a daily wage worker on other people's agricultural land. Simultaneously she studied further. In time, her husband started to ask her for money to indulge in alcohol. Vasavya Mahila Mandali helped her to stand up for herself and file a complaint in the police station. She had the courage to stand up for herself. To ensure her children had a better future. Education and employable skills are vital for financial independence.

I've met many young women who despite facing domestic violence have made a life for themselves. I'm a firm believer in 'never say never.'

My passion is social programmes for women and children. It must have shown through because my work has been valued and that has encouraged me to do more.

The best route your story can take.

To publish your own book, contact us.

We publish poetry collections, short story collections, novellas and novels.

contact@http://indiepress.in/

Instagram- indie_press